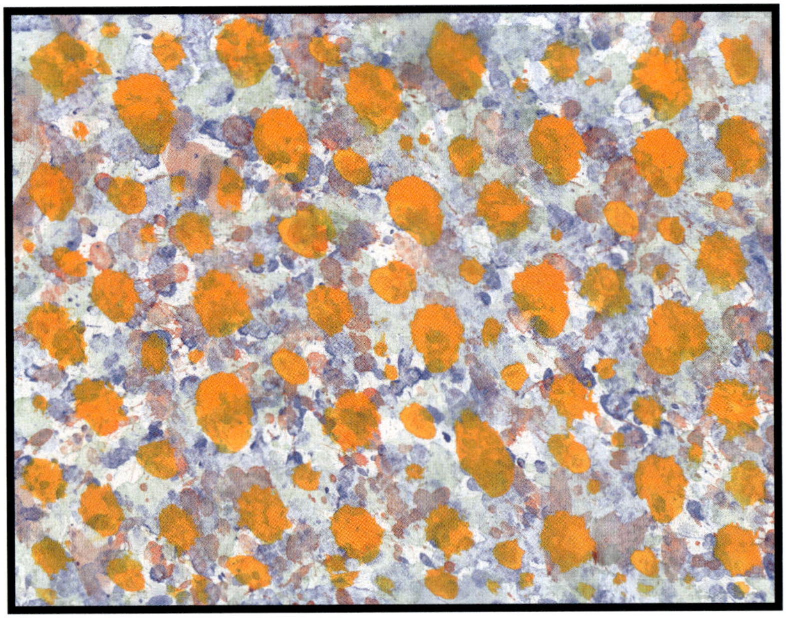

this book belongs to ______________________

Patricio

My First Art Book

cascade
social media llc

Yellow
Yellow
Yellow

Violet
Violet
Violet

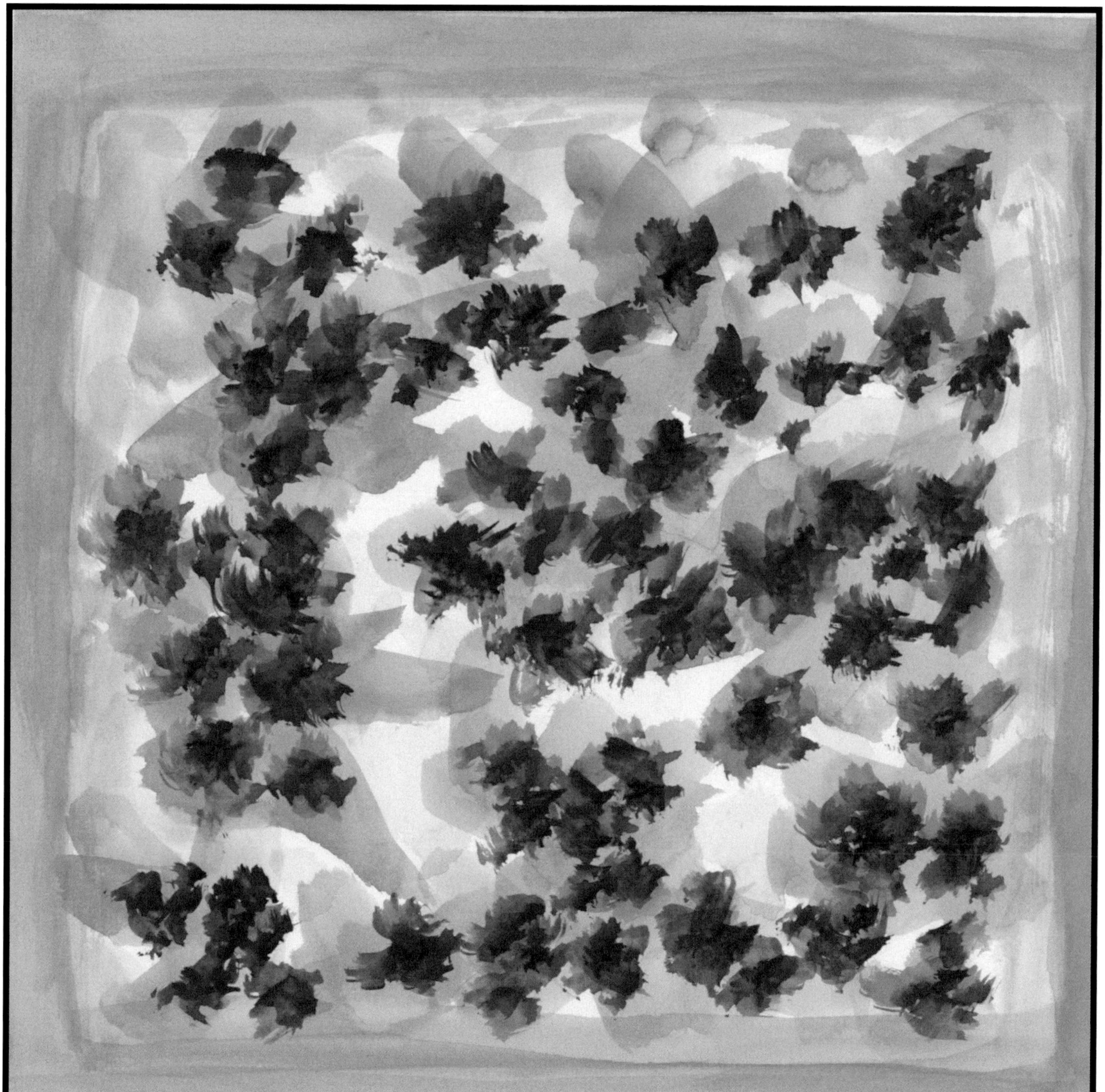

Red

Red

Red

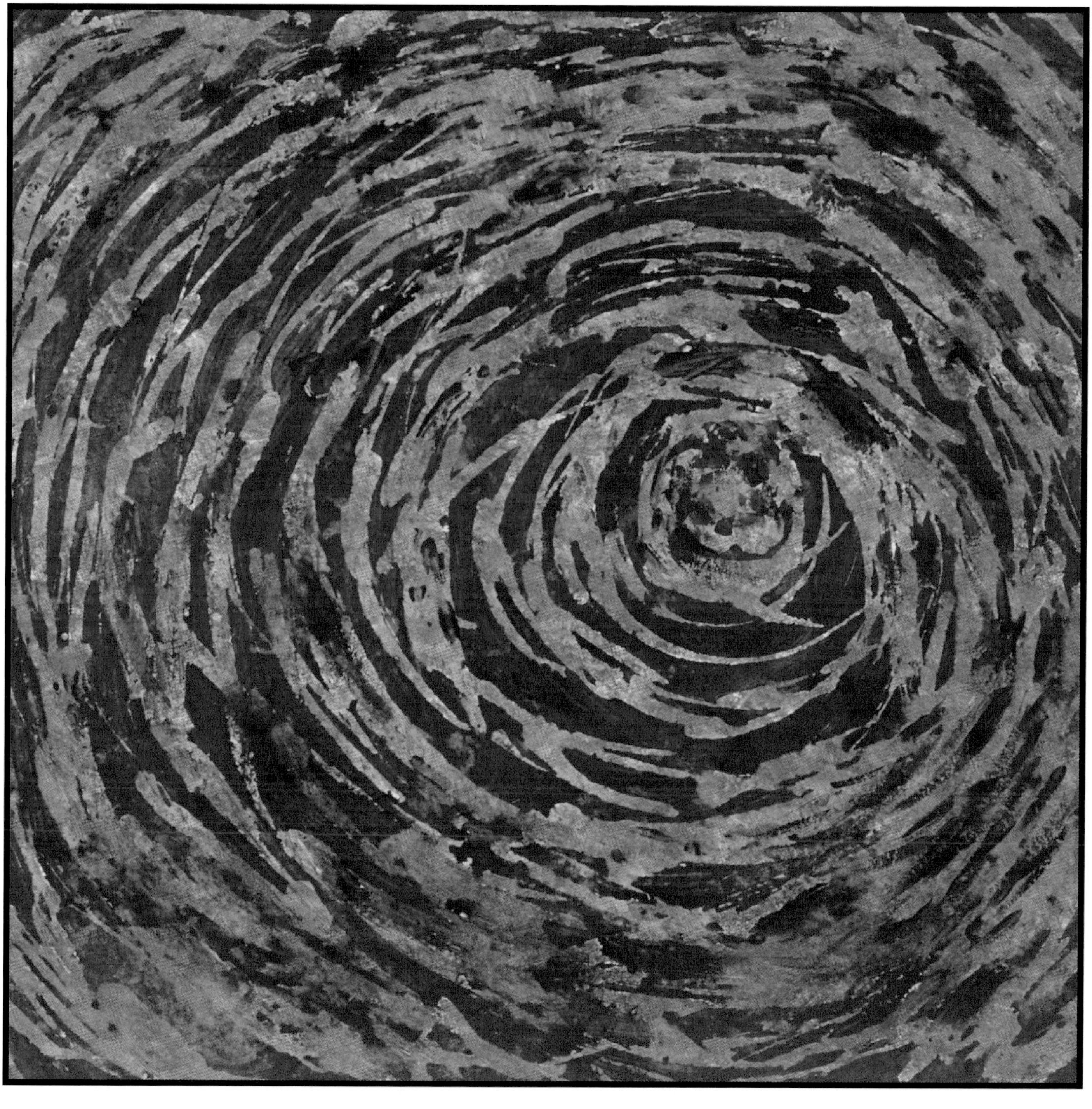

Black
Black
Black

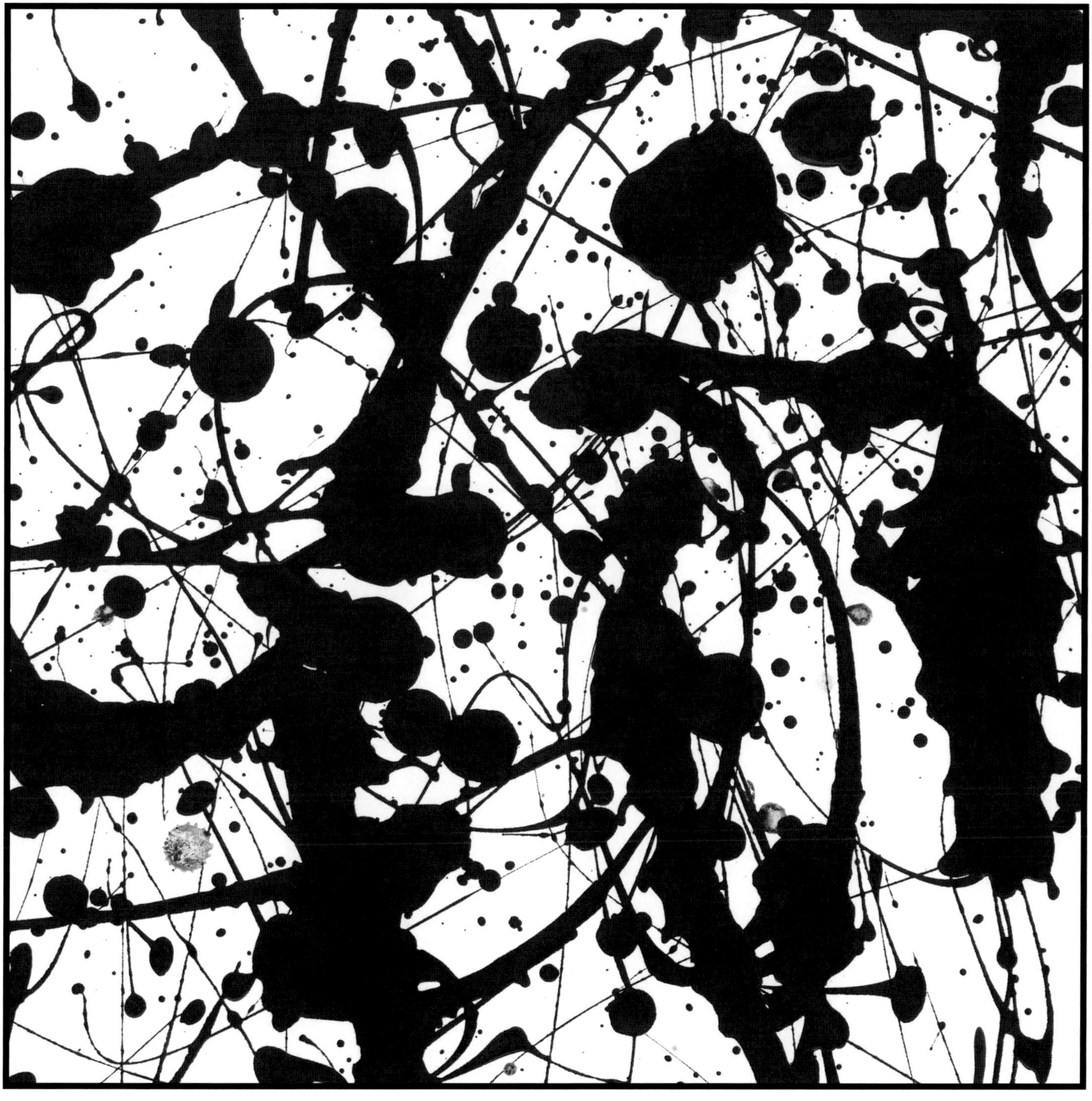

White

White

White

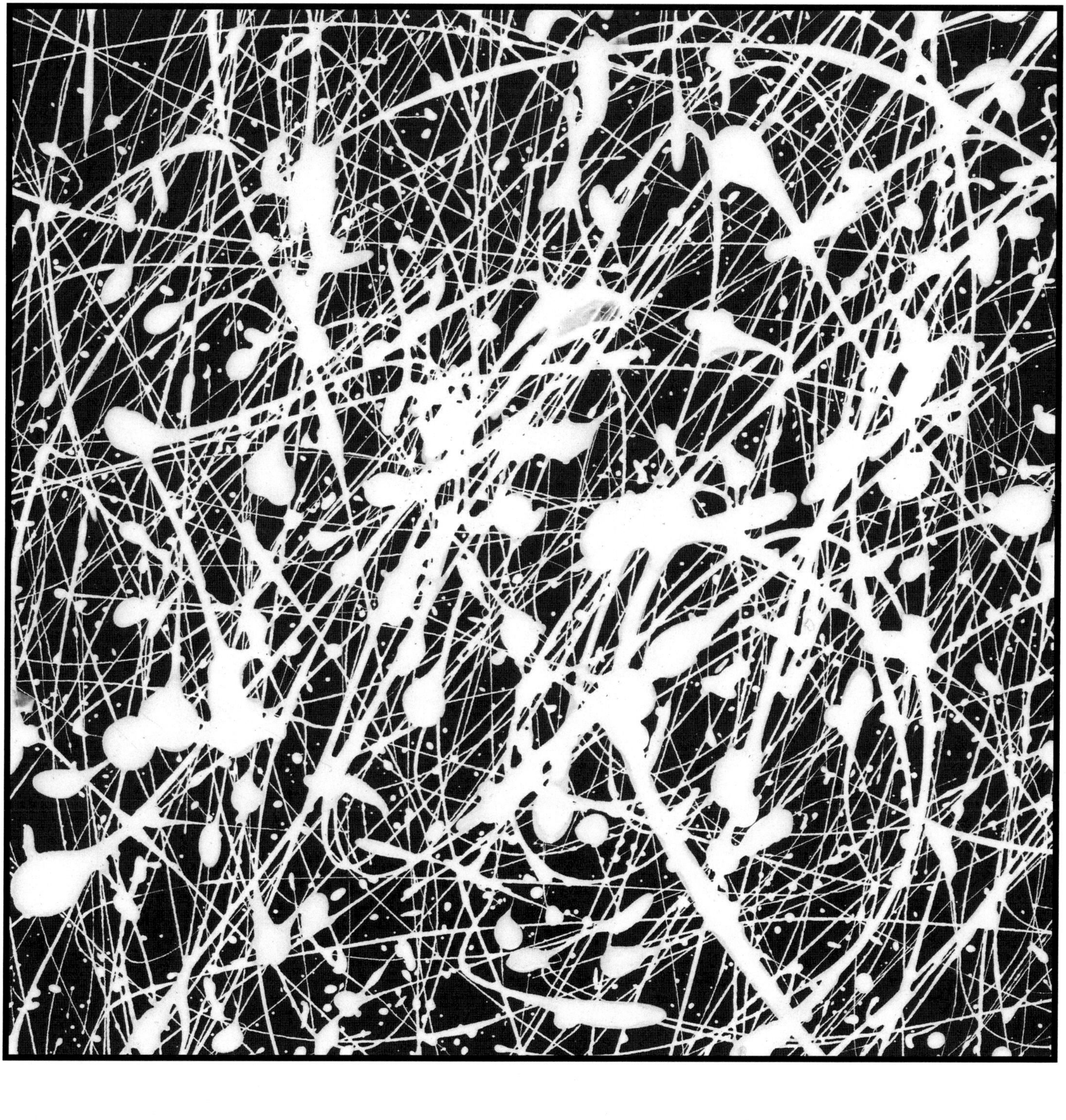

Blue

Blue

Blue

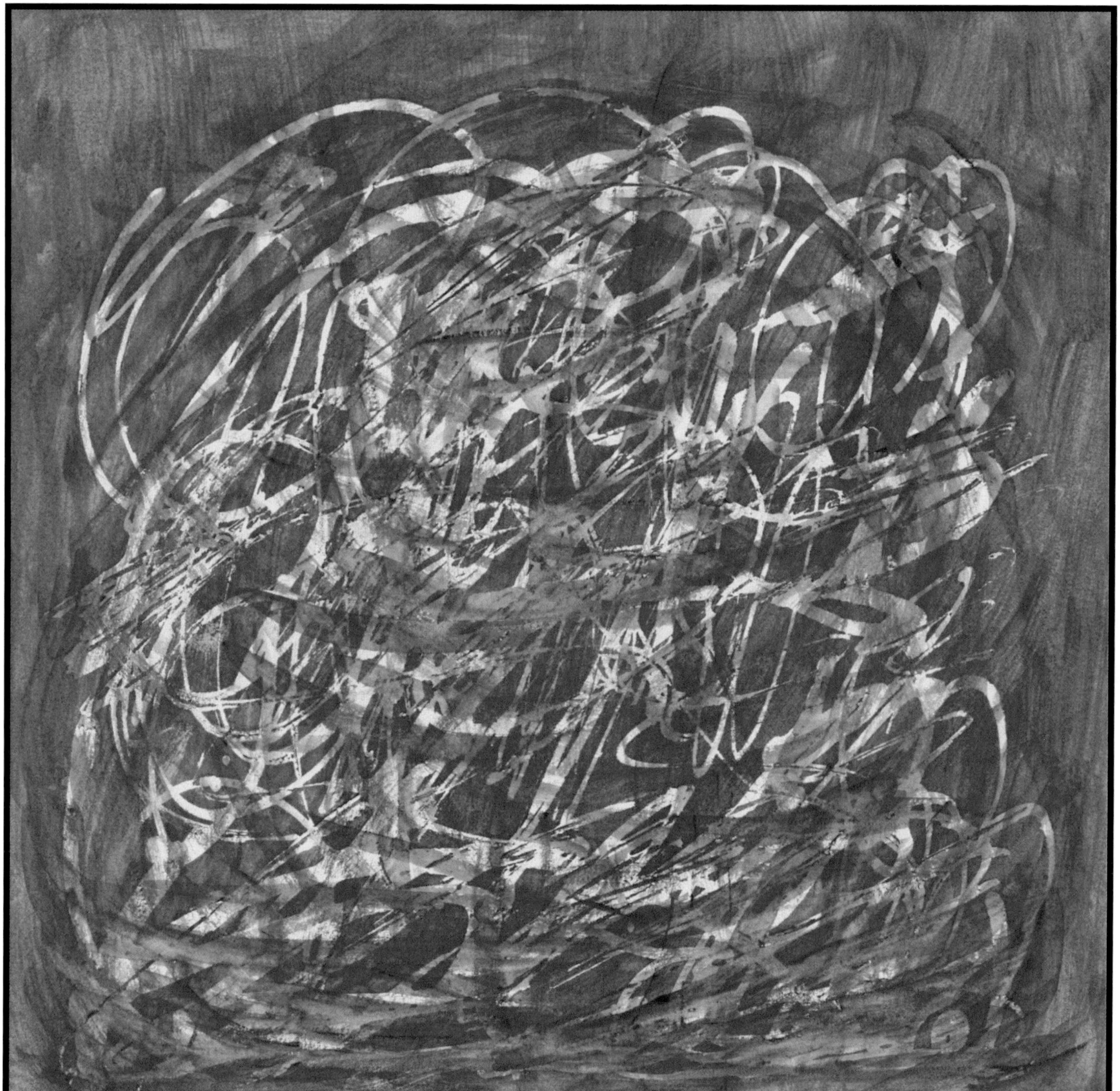

I Love You
I Love You
I Love You

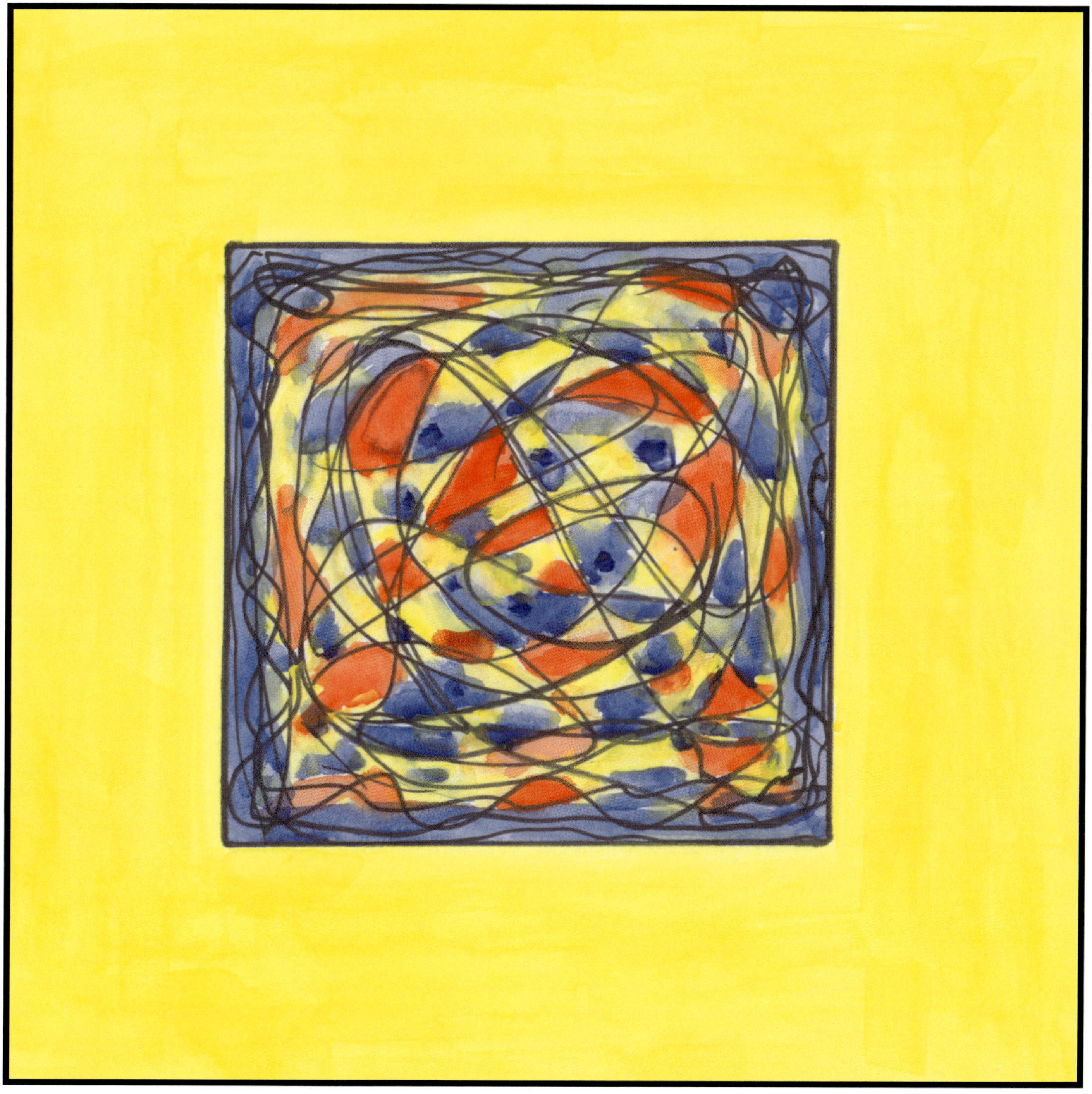

Green
Green
Green

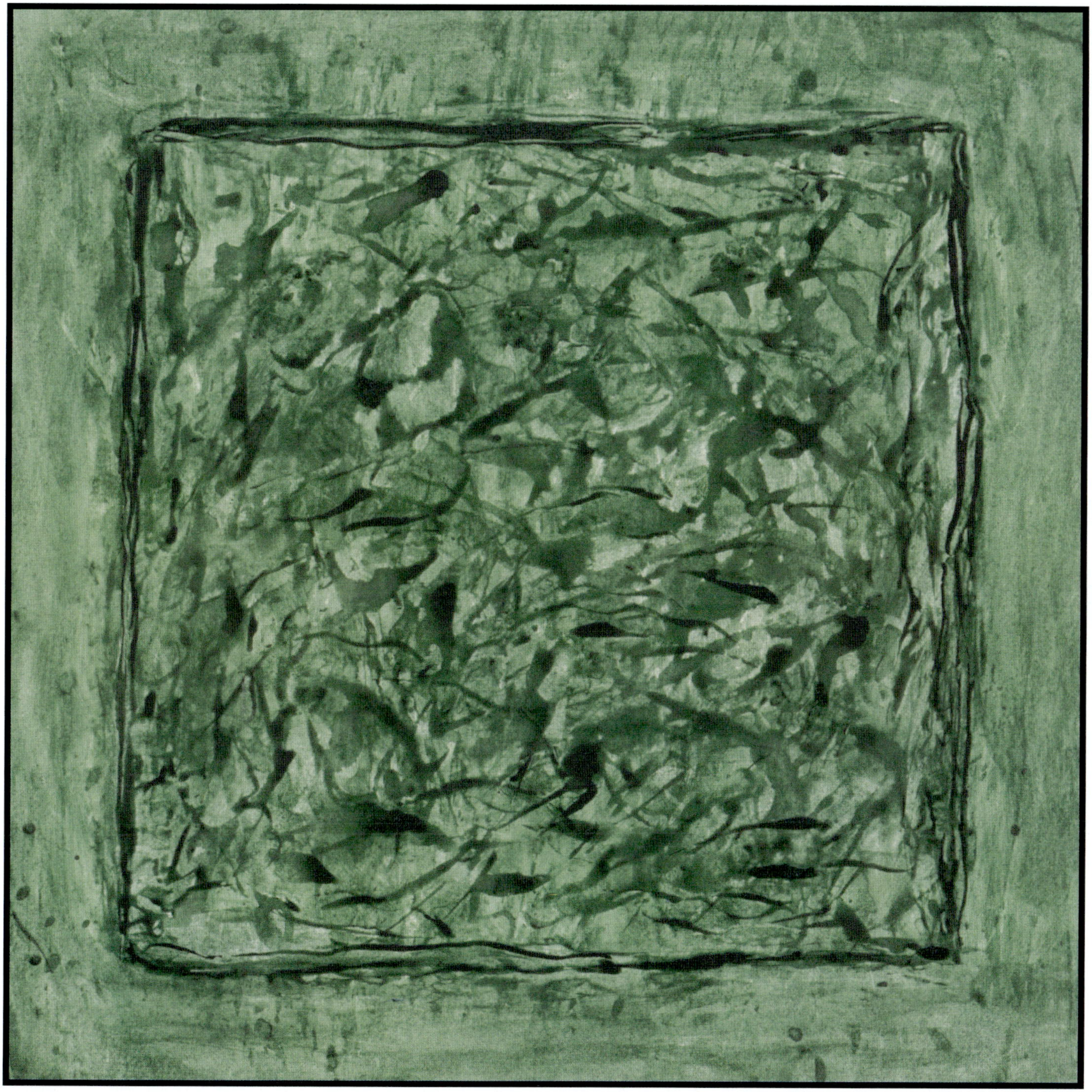

Orange
Orange
Orange

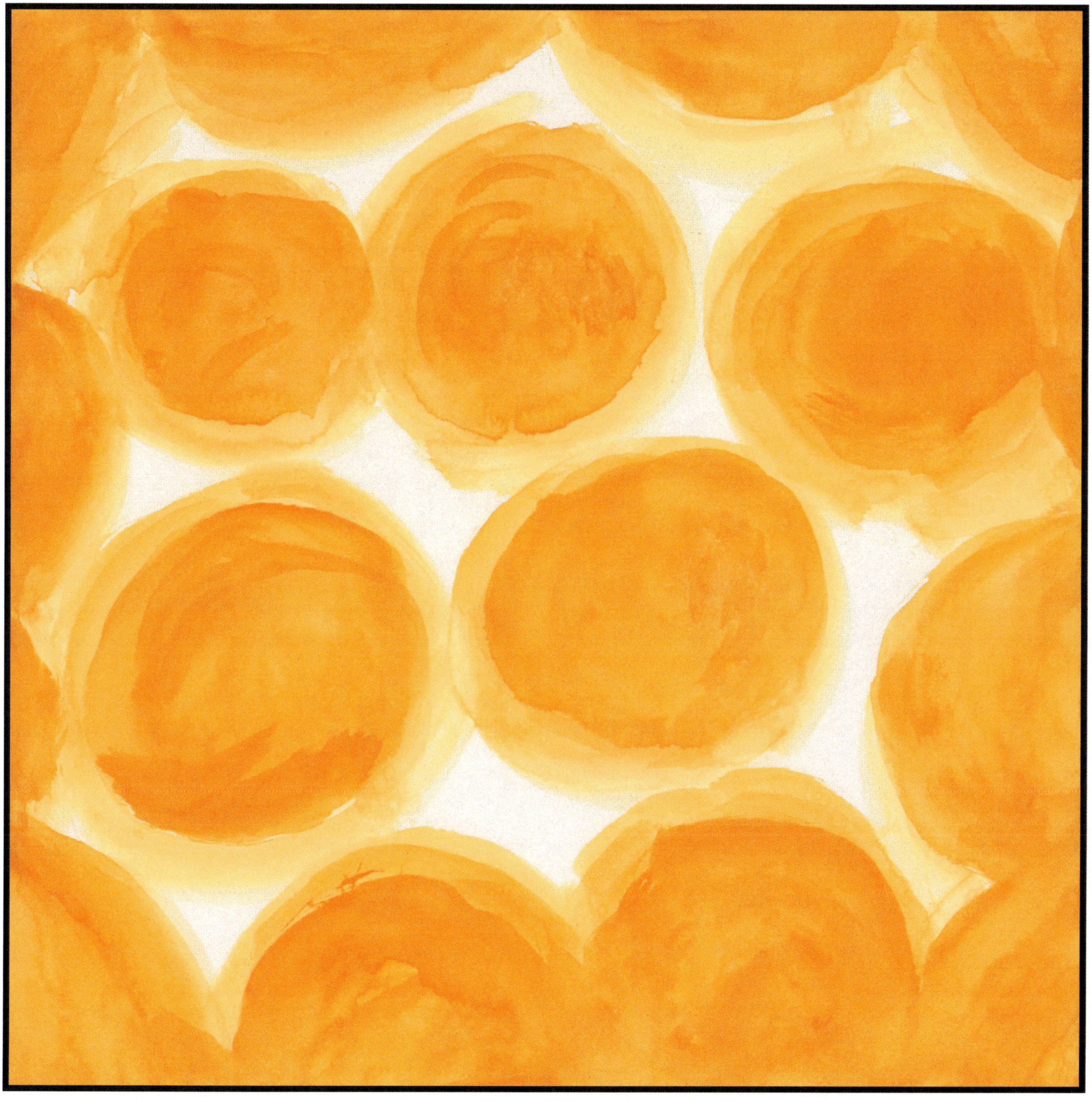

Purple
Purple
Purple

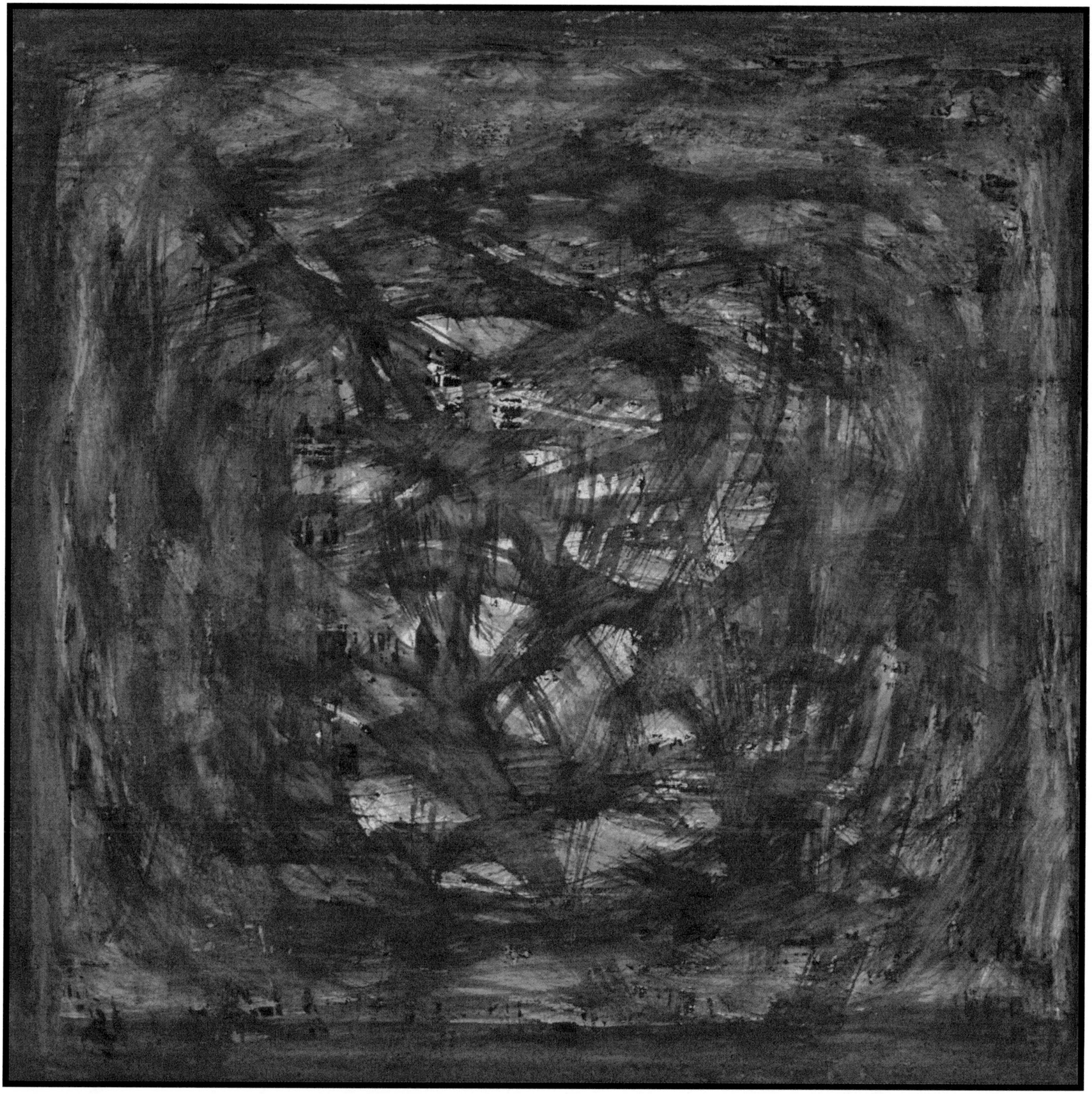

Pink
Pink
Pink

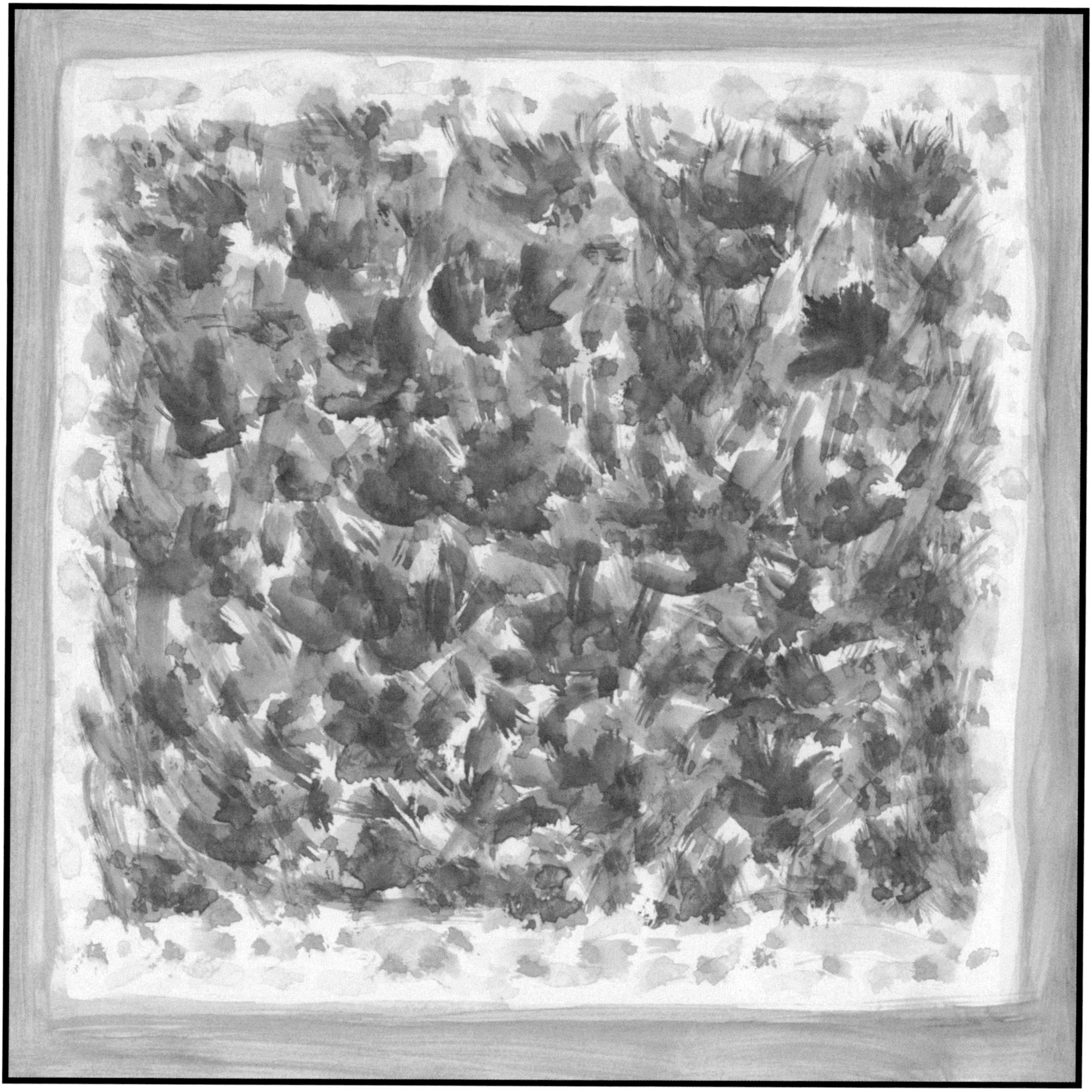

Brown

Brown

Brown

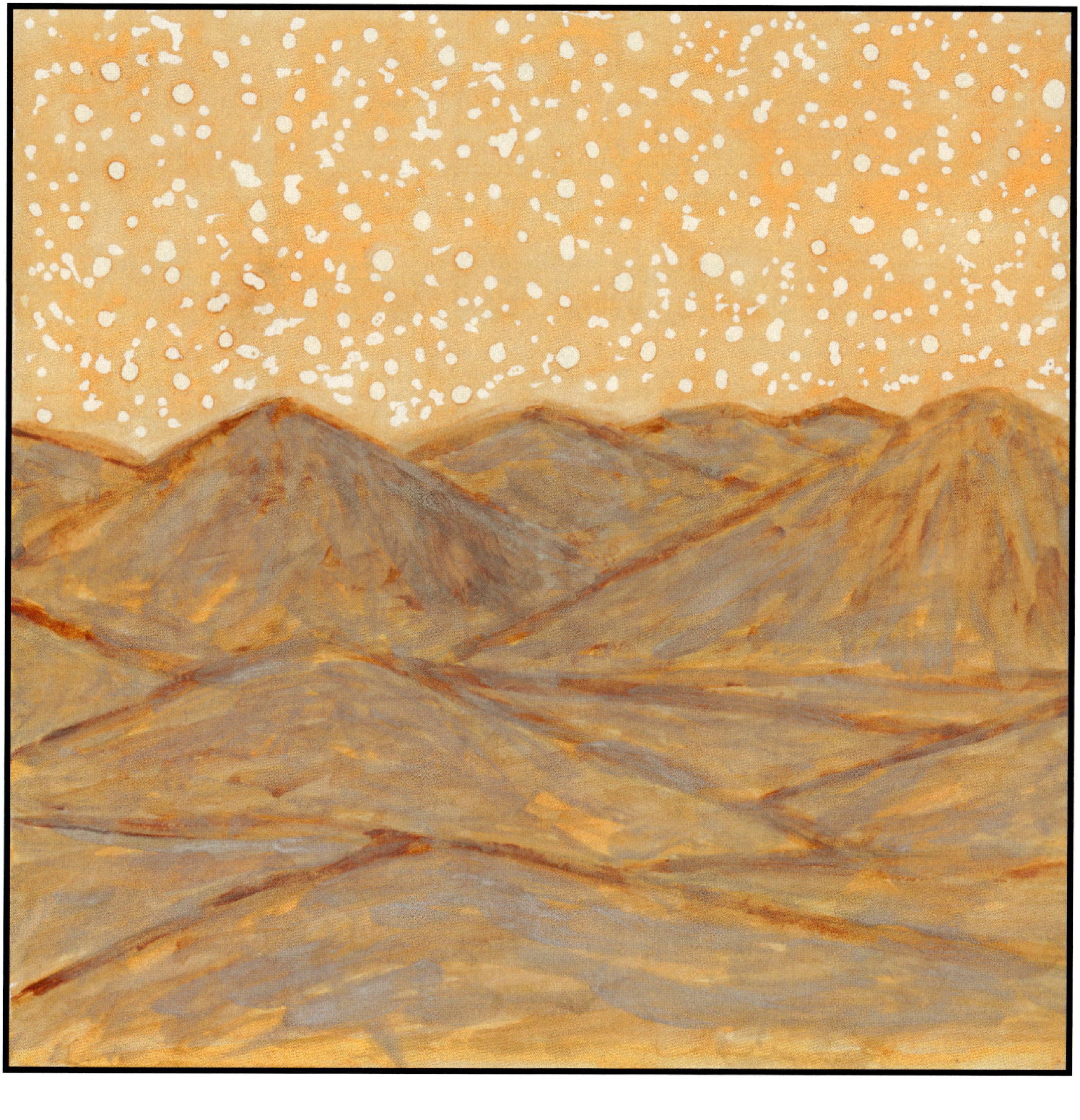

Gray

Gray

Gray

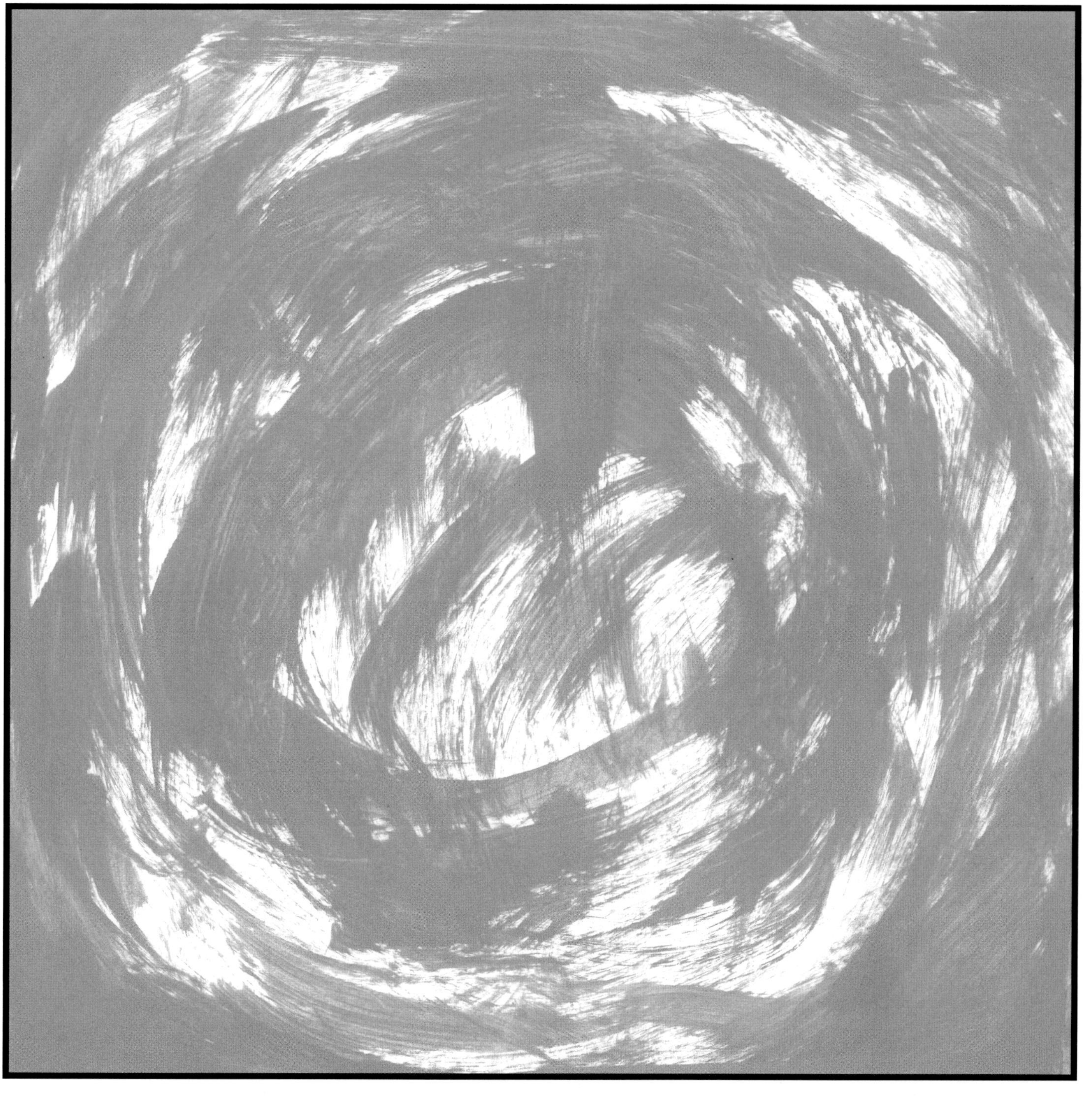

Have a
Happy Day!

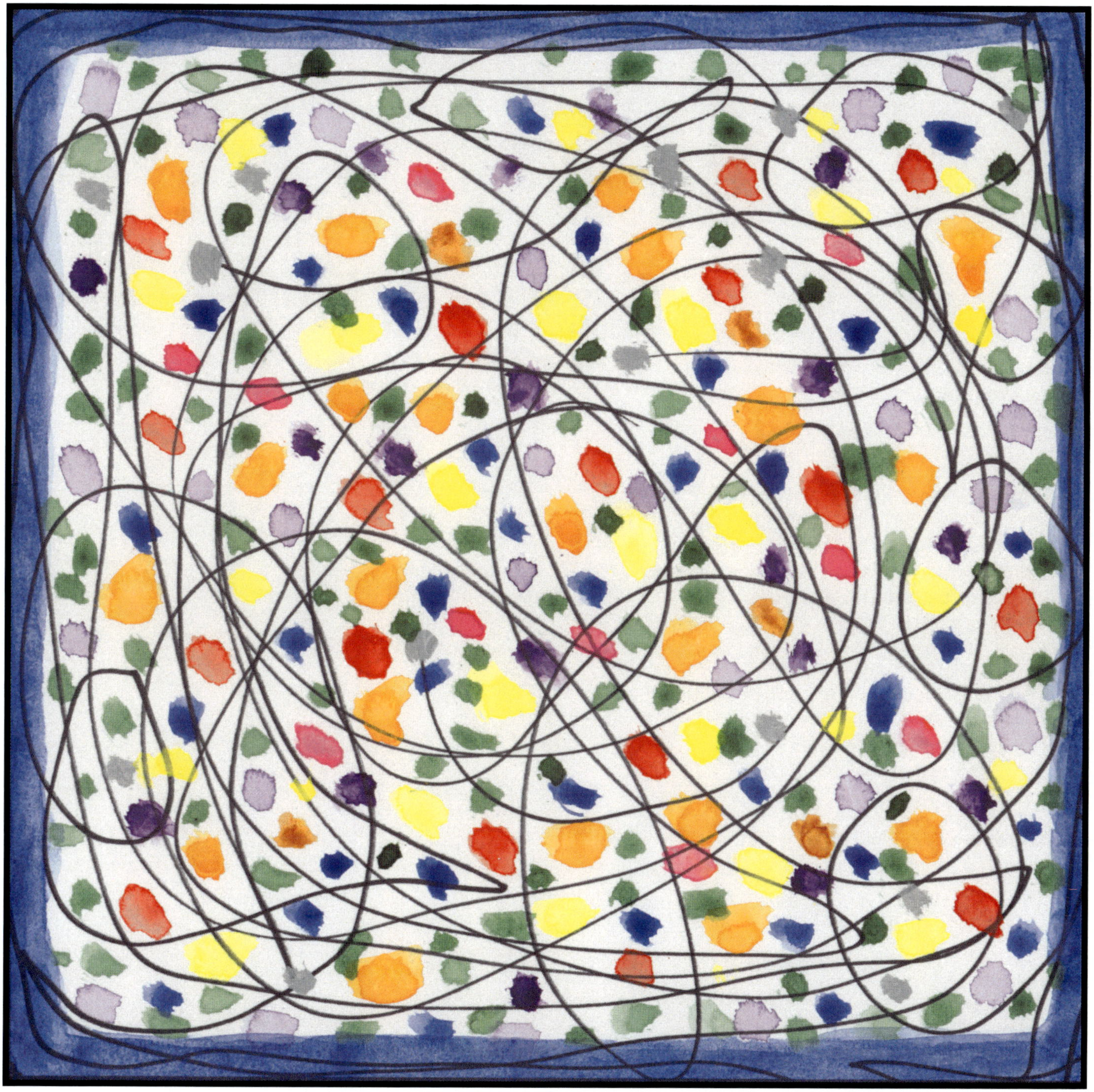

Please Visit:
Patricio.com

"My First Art Book"

Published in the United States by Cascade Social Media LLC, California
Printed in the United States of America
Patricio supports the right to read and the First Amendment.

cascade social media llc
TM Cascade Social Media LLC
ISBN 978-1-948161-99-2